CONTENTS

Introduction 5

1. The God of Word 9

2. Word and Spirit 31

3. Word and Bible 47

BRIEF BOOKS

GOD OF WORD

The Word, the Spirit and how God speaks to us

JOHN WOODHOUSE

SYDNEY · YOUNGSTOWN

God of Word
© John Woodhouse 2015

This material was first published in 1988 as a series of articles in *The Briefing*, a magazine published by Matthias Media from 1988 to 2014.

All rights reserved. Except as may be permitted by the Copyright Act, no part of this publication may be reproduced in any form or by any means without prior permission from the publisher. Please direct all copyright enquiries and permission requests to the publisher.

Matthias Media
(St Matthias Press Ltd ACN 067 558 365)
Email: info@matthiasmedia.com.au
Internet: www.matthiasmedia.com.au
Please visit our website for current postal and telephone contact information.

Matthias Media (USA)
Email: sales@matthiasmedia.com
Internet: www.matthiasmedia.com
Please visit our website for current postal and telephone contact information.

All Scripture quotations are from the Holy Bible, English Standard Version® (ESV®), copyright © 2001 by Crossway, a publishing ministry of Good News Publishers. Used by permission. All rights reserved.

ISBN 978 1 922206 83 1

Cover design and typesetting by Lankshear Design.
Series design by affiniT Design.

INTRODUCTION

Evangelicals are sometimes accused of worshipping God the Father, God the Son, and God the Holy Bible. Over the years, I've heard this criticism in many forms. For example:

- Evangelicals spend so much time studying Scripture that we don't actually live it out. All we do is talk about it, priding ourselves on our academic and intellectual rigour.
- Evangelicals focus only on the renewal of the mind, ignoring or downplaying anything to do with the heart, and with feelings and emotions. Our kind of Christianity is dry, cerebral and, frankly, boring.
- Evangelicals emphasize Scripture so much that we exclude the Holy Spirit; we don't allow room for his work in the Christian life. We don't know

what to *do* with the Spirit, so we ignore him and focus on the Bible instead.
- Evangelicals don't allow for new words from God. We are suspicious of anything that's not written down in the Bible, and so we effectively confine God's revelational power to words on a page written down centuries ago.

These kinds of arguments can leave us feeling incomplete as Christians, not to mention confused. Many of us can sense some truth in at least some of these criticisms. We can end up feeling very insecure, asking questions like:

- *Do we put too much emphasis on words?* Have I become someone who only hears the word but does not actually do it (Jas 1:22)?
- *Do we ignore matters of the heart?* Am I a joyless Christian?
- *Do we ignore the Holy Spirit?* Do I limit his work in my life?
- *Does God reveal himself in new ways today?* Does the 'word of God' equal 'the Bible'? Should I be seeking to know God through ways other than reading Scripture?

INTRODUCTION

These are all very good questions to be asking ourselves. But the insecurity provoked by these criticisms can be very harmful. It can cause faithful Christians—people who genuinely trust in the saving work of Christ—to doubt whether they are Christian at all, simply because they haven't had the same emotions or experiences as others.

So how *does* God reveal himself and how does he work in our lives? I hope this book removes any insecurity you have, and gives you confidence in your knowledge of God.

Emma Thornett
Editor

1. THE GOD OF WORD

You may have heard the complaint that, for some, Christianity has become a religion of the mind only. The problem, it is said, comes from the exclusive emphasis on the word of God. Words are rational, and by themselves words produce rationalists with a truncated view of Christianity, a limited God, a lack of openness to the fullness of God's blessings, and a religion that is discussed more than it is lived.

This objection is not without substance. There is enough truth in the description for it to be deeply disturbing to many of us.

Have we been guilty of putting undue emphasis on words? Let us look at both the Old and New Testaments to gain some perspectives on the question.

GOD OF WORD

1. God and his word in the Old Testament

There can be no argument that in the Bible the phenomenon of God's *word* is very important. We think of the psalmist, for whom the instruction ('torah') of the Lord is to be desired more than much fine gold, and is sweeter than drippings of honeycomb (Ps 19:10); we hear the voice of the prophet who declares that "the grass withers, the flower fades, but the word of our God will stand forever" (Is 40:8); and we remember that most profound description of the incarnation in the fourth gospel—"the Word became flesh and dwelt among us..." (John 1:14). Wherever we turn in the Bible we find this extraordinary phenomenon: the word of God.

Genesis 1

Perhaps we are too familiar with Genesis 1 to notice that the Bible's description of creation is striking because of this very point: God created the world by *speaking*. There were many other ways in which the ancient world thought of the gods bringing the cosmos into being. Some saw it as an emanation from the thought of the deity; others saw it as an outcome of the activity of the deity, often in battle with opponents. But the Bible says that God spoke:

1. THE GOD OF WORD

> God said, "Let there be light", and there was light.
> (Gen 1:3)

Could it be that at the very moment of the world's inception, God was indicating what kind of relationship he would have with us? As he brings the world into being, God's point of contact with his creation is his *word*. God is not found in creation itself. Neither is God so removed from creation that there is no link. His word is the link, the point of contact. The far-reaching implications of this for man's knowledge of God become clear in the course of biblical history.

Let us turn to a very clear statement still at a relatively early stage of the Bible's story.

Deuteronomy 4

A reminder of the context: Moses was in the plains of Moab on the south-east border of Canaan after the 40 years in the wilderness. The rebellious generation of Israelites he had led out of Egypt was now dead and he was addressing their children, who were poised to enter the promised land under the leadership of Joshua.

In Deuteronomy 1-3 Moses had reviewed Israel's history since Sinai, and in 4:1-8 he exhorted Israel to a life of obedience to God. Taking it up at verse 9, we should notice three things.

1. Moses addressed the new generation as if they had been at Sinai

This is a major aspect of Deuteronomy. "God dealt with you at Sinai", said Moses to those who had not even been born at the time:

> "Only take care, and keep your soul diligently, lest you forget the things that *your eyes have seen*, and lest they depart from your heart all the days of your life. Make them known to your children and your children's children—how on the day that *you stood before the* L<small>ORD</small> *your God at Horeb*, the L<small>ORD</small> said to me, 'Gather the people to me, that I may let them hear my words, so that they may learn to fear me all the days that they live on the earth, and that they may teach their children so'. And *you came near* and stood at the foot of the mountain, while the mountain burned with fire to the heart of heaven, wrapped in darkness, cloud, and gloom. Then *the* L<small>ORD</small> *spoke to you* out of the midst of the fire. *You heard* the sound of words, but saw no form; there was only a voice." (Deut 4:9-12)

This manner of speaking is exactly parallel to the New Testament statements "With Christ you died"

1. THE GOD OF WORD

(Col 2:20) and "I have been crucified with Christ" (Gal 2:20). The Israelites were *there* at Sinai in the same sense that we were *there* at the cross.

2. *The Israelites' response to God was to be fully determined by the manner in which God had dealt with them*

> "Therefore watch yourselves very carefully. Since you saw no form on the day that the Lord spoke to you at Horeb out of the midst of the fire, beware lest you act corruptly by making a carved image for yourselves, in the form of any figure, the likeness of male or female, the likeness of any animal that is on the earth, the likeness of any winged bird that flies in the air, the likeness of anything that creeps on the ground, the likeness of any fish that is in the water under the earth." (Deut 4:15-18)

God had spoken and the only valid response was to hear and heed.

This is the problem with idolatry. It is not that God is invisible and so cannot be represented visibly. The Greek Orthodox have rightly pointed out that this would deny the incarnation ("Whoever has seen me has seen the Father", said Jesus in John 14:9). The basic problem with idolatry, and this Greek

GOD OF WORD

Orthodoxy does not see, is that God has *spoken*. Making an idol is not only stupid (as the prophets delight in saying), it is corrupt, because it disregards the manner of God's dealing with us.

3. The consequences of this were radically exclusive

> "And beware lest you raise your eyes to heaven, and when you see the sun and the moon and the stars, all the host of heaven, you be drawn away and bow down to them and serve them, things that the Lord your God has allotted to all the peoples under the whole heaven. But the Lord has taken you and brought you out of the iron furnace, out of Egypt, to be a people of his own inheritance, as you are this day." (Deut 4:19-20)

We do not meet God in the sun, the moon and the stars, because these things are available to everyone everywhere. It is wrong to think that you meet God through the things he has created. This is why mysticism is also corrupt. God is met by those to whom he speaks.

The point is hammered out in the rest of the chapter. Looking forward to the time when the people would fall under God's judgement, and then return and obey him, Moses posed the Israelites a question:

1. THE GOD OF WORD

"For ask now of the days that are past, which were before you, since the day that God created man upon the earth, and ask from one end of heaven to the other, whether such a great thing as this has ever happened or was ever heard of. Did any people ever hear the voice of a god speaking out of the midst of the fire, as you have heard, and still live? Or has any god ever attempted to go and take a nation for himself from the midst of another nation, by trials, by signs, by wonders, and by war, by a mighty hand and an outstretched arm, and by great deeds of terror, all of which the Lord your God did for you in Egypt before your eyes? To you it was shown, that you might know that the Lord is God; there is no other besides him. Out of heaven he let you hear his voice, that he might discipline you. And on earth he let you see his great fire, and you heard his words out of the midst of the fire." (Deut 4:32-36)

What is the point of all this? It is that *the nature or 'shape' of our relationship with God is determined by the nature of God's revelation*. If God has approached us by speaking, then our response must have the character of hearing and heeding.

The biblical life of faith must be 'word-shaped'. This will not mean that it should be academic or unemotional or dull—absolutely on the contrary. It will mean that Christian life becomes less Christian the less it is lived out from God's word.

2. God's word and human faith

There is another angle from which we should explore this. We have seen that God approaches us with words and that this determines the kind of relationship we will have with God. What will it be like to be in a right relationship with a speaking God?

To be more specific: If God's word turns out to be a *promise*, how then should we relate to him? Will it not be by believing the promise? So it is that in both Old and New Testaments, God's word and human faith in God constitute true religion.

This is the meaning of the famous statement in Genesis 15:6, quoted by Paul in Romans 4 and Galatians 3. After Abraham expressed his difficulty in believing God's word of promise, God forcefully reiterated it:

> And he brought him outside and said, "Look toward heaven, and number the stars, if you are able to number them". Then he said to him, "So shall your offspring be". (Gen 15:5)

1. THE GOD OF WORD

Then we read:

> And he believed the Lord, and he counted it to him as righteousness. (Gen 15:6)

This statement is taken by some as suggesting that God is involved in some kind of play-acting. Abraham had faith but was a bit short on righteousness. Since he didn't have any righteousness to speak of, God pretended that his faith was righteousness. God had nothing to put in the righteousness column of his 'Abraham' ledger, so he put down his faith instead.

This view misses the point of both Genesis 15:6 and Paul's argument in Romans and Galatians. At a turning point in the history of the world, God spoke his word of promise to Abraham. And Abraham believed God. In God's estimate, that *is* righteousness. That *is* man and God rightly related. God is not a dodgy bookkeeper—if God reckons it is righteousness, it is righteousness.

Now read the story of Abraham again, and notice what creates this faith in God. It is not any virtue in Abraham for which he is rewarded with a promise. Abraham's faith is created by God, by the word of his promise. God's promise calls forth a response of trust from Abraham.

GOD OF WORD

This is precisely the point that is being made in Deuteronomy 4. In that instance, the language of obedience is used, but biblical obedience is not an antithesis to faith, any more than God's commands are in contradiction to his promises. Both are expressions of his will. God's words of command are in fact an expression of his words of promise (a point which is clear in Deuteronomy). Likewise, human obedience to the word of God is the expression of faith in the word of God.

What does this tell us? Since God has spoken, right relationship with God consists in this: *his word, and our faith in him, created by his word.* Take away his word and you have nothing. You may have superstition that pretends to be faith. You may have traditions that pretend to be Christianity. You may have religious feelings. You may have wise counselling. You may have a diary filled with good works. But without the word of God there will be no faith in God, no right relationship with God.

3. God and his word in the New Testament

Is this any different when we come to the New Testament? Now that the Word has become flesh and dwelt among us and God has poured out his

1. THE GOD OF WORD

Spirit on all mankind, has the place and character of God's word changed?

The New Testament gives an emphatic 'No'. Whatever else is overturned by the incarnation of the Son of God, whatever else can never be the same again, the manner of God's dealing with us by word is confirmed and sharpened:

> "The Spirit of the Lord is upon me... to proclaim... to proclaim... to proclaim..." (Luke 4:18-19)

> "Repentance and forgiveness of sins should be proclaimed in his name to all nations..." (Luke 24:47)

God's word to mankind is radically sharpened and clarified, and the boundaries of those addressed by God's word explode from Israel to all the nations on earth. But it does not cease to be a word.

Yes, for a brief time while Jesus was on earth there seems to have been something *more* than a word. Jesus did say, "Whoever has seen me has seen the Father" (John 14:9). Seeing Jesus is an important theme in John's Gospel, reaching its climax in chapter 20 with Thomas, for whom faith requires sight: "Unless I see... I will never believe" (John 20:25). He saw, and he believed, but Jesus' response was:

GOD OF WORD

> "Have you believed because you have seen me? Blessed are those who have not seen and yet have believed." (John 20:29)

And the writer of the gospel adds:

> Now Jesus did many other signs in the presence of the disciples, which are not written in this book; but *these are written* so that you may believe that Jesus is the Christ, the Son of God, and that believing you may have life in his name. (John 20:30-31)

And as we move from the Gospels to the book of Acts, to the epistles and into the book of Revelation, it is as clear as crystal that the word of the gospel, the word of the cross, the word of God is on centre stage. And the intended effect of that word is to bring about faith in God. Notice the note on which Acts concludes:

> [Paul] lived there two whole years at his own expense, and welcomed all who came to him, *proclaiming* the kingdom of God and *teaching* about the Lord Jesus Christ with all boldness and without hindrance. (Acts 28:30-31)

That is Christianity!

Notice the statement with which Romans begins:

1. THE GOD OF WORD

> Paul, a servant of Christ Jesus, called to be an apostle, set apart for *the gospel of God*, which he promised beforehand through his prophets in the holy Scriptures, concerning his Son, who was descended from David according to the flesh and was declared to be the Son of God in power according to the Spirit of holiness by his resurrection from the dead, Jesus Christ our Lord, through whom we have received grace and apostleship to bring about *the obedience of faith* for the sake of his name among all the nations, including you who are called to belong to Jesus Christ... (Rom 1:1-6)

What is the goal of Paul's apostleship? It is the obedience of faith among all nations. What is the means? It is the gospel about Jesus. Notice how Romans concludes:

> Now to him who is able to strengthen you according to my *gospel* and the *preaching* of Jesus Christ, according to the revelation of the mystery that was kept secret for long ages but has now been disclosed and through the prophetic writings has been made known to all nations, according to the command of the eternal God, to bring about *the obedience of faith*—to the only wise God be glory forevermore through Jesus Christ! Amen. (Rom 16:25-27)

GOD OF WORD

Notice the thematic statement of Romans:

> For I am not ashamed of *the gospel*, for it is the power of God for salvation to everyone who believes, to the Jew first and also to the Greek. For in it the righteousness of God is revealed from faith for faith, as it is written, "The righteous shall live by faith". (Rom 1:16-17)

Just as with Abraham, faith is not a sort of 'instrument', a means to some other end. The goal of the gospel in verse 16 is "for salvation"; in verse 17 the goal is "for faith". To risk labouring the point, in Romans it seems that Paul asserts that *the gospel word* and *faith in God* brought about by the gospel word is what Christianity is all about.

Let us wander through the rest of the pages of the New Testament and see if this is their story too. Many of these passages will doubtless be familiar, but look at them again. What is the place of God's word in their thinking?

1. THE GOD OF WORD

Is the New Testament 'word-shaped'?

For Christ did not send me to baptize but to *preach the gospel*, and not with words of eloquent wisdom, lest the cross of Christ be emptied of its power.

For *the word of the cross* is folly to those who are perishing, but to us who are being saved it is the power of God. (1 Cor 1:17-18)

Therefore, having this ministry by the mercy of God, we do not lose heart. But we have renounced disgraceful, underhanded ways. We refuse to practice cunning or to tamper with *God's word*, but by *the open statement of the truth* we would commend ourselves to everyone's conscience in the sight of God. (2 Cor 4:1-2)

O foolish Galatians! Who has bewitched you? It was before your eyes that Jesus Christ was publicly portrayed as crucified. Let me ask you only this: Did you receive the Spirit by works of the law or by *hearing with faith*? (Gal 3:1-2)

In him you also, when you *heard the word of truth*, *the gospel of your salvation*, and believed in him, were sealed with the promised Holy Spirit… (Eph 1:13)

GOD OF WORD

I want you to know, brothers, that what has happened to me has really served to advance *the gospel*... And most of the brothers, having become confident in the Lord by my imprisonment, are much more bold to speak *the word* without fear...

What then? Only that in every way, whether in pretense or in truth, Christ is proclaimed, and in that I rejoice. (Phil 1:12, 14, 18)

We always thank God, the Father of our Lord Jesus Christ, when we pray for you, since we heard of your faith in Christ Jesus and of the love that you have for all the saints, because of the hope laid up for you in heaven. Of this you have heard before in *the word of the truth, the gospel, which has come to you*, as indeed in the whole world it is bearing fruit and increasing—as it also does among you, since the day you heard it and understood the grace of God in truth... (Col 1:3-6)

And we also thank God constantly for this, that when you received *the word of God*, which you heard from us, you accepted it not as the word of men, but as what it really is, *the word of God*, which is at work in you believers. (1 Thess 2:13)

1. THE GOD OF WORD

To this he called you through our *gospel*, so that you may obtain the glory of our Lord Jesus Christ. So then, brothers, stand firm and hold to *the traditions that you were taught by us, either by our spoken word or by our letter...*

Finally, brothers, pray for us, that *the word of the Lord* may speed ahead and be honoured, as it happened among you. (2 Thess 2:14-15, 3:1)

Until I come, devote yourself to the public *reading of Scripture*, to *exhortation*, to *teaching*. (1 Tim 4:13)

Do your best to present yourself to God as one approved, a worker who has no need to be ashamed, rightly handling *the word of truth*. (2 Tim 2:15)

[An overseer] must hold firm to *the trustworthy word* as taught, so that he may be able to give instruction in sound doctrine and also to rebuke those who contradict it. (Titus 1:9)

Long ago, at many times and in many ways, God spoke to our forefathers by the prophets, but in these last days *he has spoken to us* by his Son... (Heb 1:1-2)

GOD OF WORD

For *the word of God* is living and active, sharper than any two-edged sword, piercing to the division of soul and spirit, of joints and of marrow, and discerning the thoughts and intentions of the heart. (Heb 4:12)

Of his own will he brought us forth by *the word of truth*, that we should be a kind of firstfruits of his creatures. (Jas 1:18)

...since you have been born again, not of perishable seed but of imperishable, through the living and abiding *word of God*; for

> "All flesh is like grass,
>   and all its glory like the flower of grass.
> The grass withers,
>   and the flower falls,
> but *the word of the Lord* remains forever."

And *this word is the good news that was preached to you*. (1 Pet 1:23-25)

...that which we have seen and heard *we proclaim* also to you, so that you too may have fellowship with us; and indeed our fellowship is with the Father and with his Son Jesus Christ. (1 John 1:3)

1. THE GOD OF WORD

> Everyone who goes on ahead and does not abide in *the teaching of Christ*, does not have God. Whoever abides in the teaching has both the Father and the Son. (2 John 9)
>
> For I rejoiced greatly when the brothers came and testified to your truth, as indeed you are walking in *the truth*. I have no greater joy than to hear that my children are walking in *the truth*. (3 John 3-4)
>
> He who has an ear, let him hear *what the Spirit says* to the churches. (Rev 2:7)

We might crystallize the point of all this in a simple proposition: *Where you have the word of God creating faith in God* (and nothing else can create real faith in God) *there is all of biblical Christianity*. Where the word of God is lacking there is no Christianity.

What does this mean for the accusation that evangelical Christianity with its emphasis on words has become an intellectual's religion? There is, I suspect, some truth in the accusation. However, it is one thing to recognize that our faith and life are less than they ought to be. It is another thing to blame that inadequacy on a particular doctrinal emphasis.

GOD OF WORD

Noticing symptoms is one thing; diagnosis is another; and prescription is another again.

If our Christianity has become too cerebral it is not because of an emphasis on words. Words are not the property of intellectuals. To quote Moses:

> For this commandment that I command you today is not too hard for you, neither is it far off. It is not in heaven, that you should say, "Who will ascend to heaven for us and bring it to us, that we may hear it and do it?" Neither is it beyond the sea, that you should say, "Who will go over the sea for us and bring it to us, that we may hear it and do it?" But the word is very near you. It is in your mouth and in your heart, so that you can do it. (Deut 30:11-14)

What was true of the word of God then is true of the gospel word. It is not the prerogative of intellectuals. It is near to all of us:

> But the righteousness based on faith says, "Do not say in your heart, 'Who will ascend into heaven?'" (that is, to bring Christ down) "or 'Who will descend into the abyss?'" (that is, to bring Christ up from the dead). But what does it say? "The word is near you, in your mouth and in your heart" (that is, the word of faith that we proclaim); because, if you confess with your mouth that Jesus

1. THE GOD OF WORD

> is Lord and believe in your heart that God raised him from the dead, you will be saved. (Rom 10:6-9)

The answer to the error of intellectualizing Christianity is not to change its fundamental word character, but to ensure that we do not obscure or complicate or add to the word of God. We must not seek a level of experience other than faith in God created by the word of God. We need to preach and teach God's word so that every obstacle to the knowledge of God is destroyed (even the obstacle of anti-intellectualism), and every thought taken captive to obey Christ (cf. 2 Cor 10:5).

Evangelical ministry must be flexible and adaptable and imaginative and inventive as far as manner and style goes. But there is simply no liberty for it to be other than ministry of the word of God:

> Him we proclaim, warning everyone and teaching everyone with all wisdom, that we may present everyone mature in Christ. For this I toil, struggling with all his energy that he powerfully works within me. (Col 1:28-29)

4. Conclusion

It is this that distinguishes evangelical Christianity from all other forms of Christianity. It is what makes evangelical Christianity not one Christian party among many, but authentic Christianity. Giving due emphasis to the word of God is not only the touchstone for evangelical ministry, it is the point of reference for all our failings.

If our Christianity has become dry and dull and dead, it will be because the word of God does not occupy the place it should. If our churches have become closed cliques with no concern for society and the world around us, it will be because the word of God does not occupy the place it should. If we have become prayerless, it will be because the word of God does not occupy the place it should.

It is not that evangelicals emphasize the word of God while Catholics emphasize sacraments and charismatics emphasize the Holy Spirit and liberals emphasize good works and Anglicans keep it all in balance! The word of God is not just the evangelical party flag, some arbitrary element that is our particular hobby horse.

Our whole practice and experience of Christianity flows from this reality: that *God has spoken*. Everything—and I mean everything—is a consequence of that reality.

2. WORD AND SPIRIT

There is a strange criticism sometimes levelled at certain kinds of Christians: "They are too experiential". I think I know what is meant, but what a strange way to put it—as though we can have too much 'experience'. It's a little like saying, "That person breathes too much". Should there be, or can there be, some limit placed on our experience of God?

My argument in the previous chapter might be misunderstood to be arguing against experience in the Christian life. Nothing could be further from the truth.

The Christian life is characterized by deep and profound experiences, so much so that in New Testament times the Christians were often described with reference to the distinctive experiences that marked them out. There are several expressions like this in the New Testament. One of them is 'the called ones' or 'those who are called'. For the Christians, the experience of having been *called* was so distinctive and all-embracing that it identified them. The reference is, of course, to being called by God through the gospel word—called to God himself. What an experience that is: to have heard the gospel, and to have realized that you were not being addressed by man but by God himself!

Do you know that experience? If you do, then don't accuse others of having too much experience.

There is another very wonderful, and apparently favourite, expression for Christians in the New Testament that refers to them by a characteristic experience. Christians are called 'believers'. They are people who have this experience: faith in God. They have been addressed by God, and what God has said to them has brought them to this experience of 'trust' or 'belief'. What an experience! Is there any other to match it? Can we have too much of it?

Word vs Spirit?

In the previous chapter, I came to the point of saying that *where there is the word of God, and faith in God because of that word, there is the totality of*

2. WORD AND SPIRIT

Christianity. Is this anti-experiential? No, for it focuses on the central definitive experience of the Christian life.

In this chapter we will look at a common objection to this thesis: that this narrow emphasis on *word* is at the expense of the *Spirit*. It is argued that the arid tedium of much evangelical Christianity is seen right here: the emphasis on word has produced a religion of the mind only. Our preachers are lecturers (with all the dullness that implies) and our Bible studies are literary seminars. Surely there is more to Christianity than just words?

It is an objection that is not without substance, and it comes from people who themselves uphold the reality and power of God's word. They would offer little objection to anything I have said thus far, except to its exclusiveness, its narrowness. They would object, in other words, not to what I have said; only to what I have left unsaid. It would be agreed that wherever there is genuine Christianity there will certainly be the word of God and faith in God. That is necessary... but it is not all. It is not adequate. It is not sufficient.

When this inadequacy is felt (as I believe it is being felt by many today), Christian ministries begin to take on a new shape. The Christian life begins to develop in a new way. There is, of course, a word dimension, but people begin to seek the missing Spirit dimension. These may not be completely unrelated, but they are nevertheless viewed as distinct and different. The minister still studies his Bible and preaches it—of course—but he is also 'led by the Spirit', which is something distinct. The Christian person still reads their Bible and listens to sermons, but there is another experience sought after: an encounter with the Spirit.

An increasing number of Christian meetings are being structured round these two distinct dimensions of Christian experience. There is the reading of the Bible with the sermon, and then there is a quite separate time when the Spirit of God is expected to do something more. It has been described to me like this:

> Of course God meets us in his word. But that is not the only way in which he deals with us. There is another dimension, a more direct working of God—almost a more tangible working, by his Spirit.

I want to suggest that this line of thinking, and the implications it has for Christian life and ministry, are mistaken in a most serious way.

2. WORD AND SPIRIT

Just words?

Before expanding on this, it needs to be said that it is certainly possible to have an emphasis on words (even the words of the Bible) that is inadequate.

I can study the historical and cultural background of the letters to the seven churches; I can explain the literary structure of the letter to the Romans; I can weave jokes and illustrations around a passage from the Gospels; I can talk about the meanings of Greek and Hebrew words. And they can all have to do with the Bible. But I have not necessarily encountered, nor conveyed, the word *of God*. All those things can aid understanding the word of God, but they are not themselves the word of God. God's word is simply what *God* has said.

There are times when evangelicals fall into this error of studying the words of the Bible *for their own sake*. If we separate the words from the Speaker and give them autonomy, we have missed the point of Bible study entirely. (There are schools of modern literary criticism which insist on doing just that, and must therefore be regarded as inadequate approaches to the Bible.) The words of the Bible matter, but only because they are the words *of God*.

GOD OF WORD

Word *and* Spirit

Having made that qualification, let us look at the connection between God's *Spirit* and God's *word* in the Bible. One problem for us in understanding this connection is that English lacks a word which has the range of meaning of the Hebrew *ruach* and the Greek *pneuma*. Both of these words can mean 'breath' as well as 'spirit'. Throughout the Bible, the Spirit of God is as closely connected to the word of God as *breath* is connected to *speech*. The connection is suggested in the very first words of Genesis:

> In the beginning, God created the heavens and the earth. The earth was without form and void, and darkness was over the face of the deep; and the *Spirit [breath] of God* was hovering over the face of the waters. And God *said*, "Let there be light", and there was light. (Gen 1:1-3)

The *breath* of God took the form of *speech*.

Skipping past generations of Old Testament history, we also find the connection in the prophecy of Isaiah:

> And the Spirit [breath] of the Lord shall rest upon him,
>   the Spirit [breath] of wisdom and understanding,
>   the Spirit [breath] of counsel and might,

2. WORD AND SPIRIT

> the Spirit [breath] of knowledge and the fear
> of the Lord. (Isa 11:2)

See how close the attributes of the Spirit are to the attributes of the word of God: wisdom, understanding, counsel, knowledge.

More clearly still, consider Isaiah 59:21:

> "And as for me, this is my covenant with them", says the Lord: "My Spirit [breath] that is upon you, and my words that I have put in your mouth, shall not depart out of your mouth, or out of the mouth of your offspring, or out of the mouth of your children's offspring", says the Lord, "from this time forth and forevermore".

Here it is not too much to say that "my Spirit that is upon you" and "my words that I have put in your mouth" are the same thing. They are used interchangeably. The connection is maintained in the very important text of Isaiah 61:1:

> The Spirit [breath] of the Lord God is upon me,
>   because the Lord has anointed me
> to bring good news to the poor…

Notice the 'because'. Jesus quotes this prophecy in Luke 4:18:

GOD OF WORD

> "The Spirit of the Lord is upon me,
> *because* he has anointed me
> to proclaim good news to the poor."

This is the same as saying: "He has anointed me to proclaim good news *therefore* the Spirit of the Lord is upon me".

Where the word of God is, there the Spirit or breath of God is also. Word and breath cannot be separated. The connection flows on into the New Testament:

> "Behold, I am sending you out as sheep in the midst of wolves, so be wise as serpents and innocent as doves. Beware of men, for they will deliver you over to courts and flog you in their synagogues, and you will be dragged before governors and kings for my sake, to bear witness before them and the Gentiles. When they deliver you over, do not be anxious how you are to speak or what you are to say, for what you are to say will be given to you in that hour. For it is not you who speak, but the Spirit [breath] of your Father speaking through you." (Matt 10:16-20)

What will the Spirit do? *Speak* through the testimony of the disciples to Jesus—through the gospel they will speak. Note also the famous statement in Acts 1:8:

2. WORD AND SPIRIT

> "But you will receive power when the Holy Spirit has come upon you, and you will be my witnesses in Jerusalem and in all Judea and Samaria, and to the end of the earth."

What will happen with the coming of the Spirit? The disciples will bear witness to Jesus. They will speak the gospel. See it happening again in Acts 5:30-32:

> "The God of our fathers raised Jesus, whom you killed by hanging him on a tree. God exalted him at his right hand as Leader and Saviour, to give repentance to Israel and forgiveness of sins. And we are witnesses to these things, and so is the Holy Spirit, whom God has given to those who obey him."

The gospel they preach is not only their testimony, but the testimony of the Holy Spirit, the holy breath of God:

> For we know, brothers loved by God, that he has chosen you, because our gospel came to you not only in word, but also in power and in the Holy Spirit and with full conviction. You know what kind of men we proved to be among you for your sake. And you became imitators of us and of the Lord, for you received the word in much affliction, with the joy of the Holy Spirit... (1 Thess 1:4-6)

GOD OF WORD

Are there two things going on here—"not only in word, but also in power and in the Holy Spirit"? No, he is describing one experience: what they experienced when "our gospel came". The gospel is never just words.

Exactly the same point is made in the next chapter:

> And we also thank God constantly for this, that when you received the word of God, which you heard from us, you accepted it not as the word of men but as what it really is, the word of God, which is at work in you believers. (1 Thess 2:13)

The gospel comes in power and in the Holy Spirit precisely because it is the word *of God*. And notice, too, that Paul says that God is at work in you who believe. How is God at work? 'By his Spirit' would be a thoroughly Pauline way of putting it, but here he says it is the word of God that is at work. Is there a difference? I suggest not. It is by his word that God's Spirit is at work.

We will understand the work of the Spirit of God in the New Testament, and in our lives, only when we see the inseparable connection between God's Spirit and God's word—when we see, as Paul puts it in Ephesians 6:17, that the sword of the Spirit is the word of God.

2. WORD AND SPIRIT

There are many statements in the New Testament where 'Spirit' and 'word' are virtually interchangeable. When James says that God "brought us forth by the word of truth" (Jas 1:18), would he have been saying something very different if he had said, "God brought us forth by the work of his Spirit"?

Peter says:

> ...since you have been born again, not of perishable seed but of imperishable, through the living and abiding word of God... (1 Pet 1:23)

Is he speaking of something different from Jesus?

> Jesus answered, "Truly, truly, I say to you, unless one is born of water and the Spirit, he cannot enter the kingdom of God". (John 3:5)

Jesus said of the Holy Spirit:

> "And when he comes, he will convict the world concerning sin and righteousness and judgement: concerning sin, because they do not believe in me; concerning righteousness, because I go to the Father, and you will see me no longer; concerning judgement, because the ruler of this world is judged." (John 16:8-11)

GOD OF WORD

Was he speaking of something other than what would happen through the proclamation of the gospel? No. The Spirit is the Spirit of truth (John 16:13) who will lead us into all truth, and this truth is the gospel—as Jesus said, "he will bear witness about me" (John 15:26).

Conclusion

Let me return to our proposition: *Where there is the word of God, and faith in God because of that word, there is the totality of Christianity.*

There is a danger in this proposition. It can be misunderstood as: *Where there are words* **about** *God and some kind of assent to the words, there is Christianity.* And perhaps some of our Christianity has become like that. Certainly, you can have ten thousand words about God and not have Christianity. That is not what I am saying.

Where there is the word *of God*, there certainly is the Holy Spirit. After all, it is his sword. The Christian life is fully lived in the power of the Spirit, not when something additional to the word of God is discovered and called a spiritual gift, but when, and only when, the word of God is at work in you who believe—when God, by his Spirit, *addresses* us and we receive *his* word.

2. WORD AND SPIRIT

Further thoughts: The subjective work of the Spirit

> *You ask me how I know he lives?*
> *He lives within my heart!*[1]

So the old chorus goes. But have Christians gone too far in subjectivizing the work of the Holy Spirit? Romans 8:16 is a favourite verse in this area:

> The Spirit himself bears witness with our spirit that we are children of God...

Like many New Testament statements, this refers to the subjective *effect* of the Spirit's work. The question, however, remains—*how* does the Spirit bear witness to me? The answer is: by the gospel, by the word of God.

Evangelicals have often failed to understand this, and in effect have believed in two sources of revelation. This criticism was levelled at the 16th-century Reformers. According to the Roman Catholics, the Reformers had simply

---
1 'I Serve a Risen Saviour', AH Ackley, 1933.

replaced the twin authorities of Scripture and Tradition with Scripture and the subjective testimony of the Spirit. Catholic theology would argue: "How do I know the Bible is God's word? The church tells me. Why is it better to say 'I know it in my heart'? How can you be certain that the testimony in your heart is the work of God's Spirit? Might not the testimony of God's church be the work of his Spirit?"

However, I believe (although it is a matter of debate) that these critics had misunderstood the Reformers. The Reformers were not speaking about two revelations from God—one, objective in the Bible (saying 'Jesus Christ is Lord') and another, subjective in your heart (saying 'The Bible is *my* word'). Rather, they would have affirmed that the objective word that Jesus is Lord comes with the power of God's Spirit, exactly because it is the word *of God*. God *breathes* that word to me and by it creates faith in him—just as he did with Abraham. It is one work, not two:

2. WORD AND SPIRIT

> For God, who said, "Let light shine out of darkness", has shone in our hearts to give the light of the knowledge of the glory of God in the face of Jesus Christ. (2 Cor 4:6)
>
> That is the work of God's Spirit—it is the work of the gospel word.

3. WORD AND BIBLE

Here is our proposition once more: *Where there is the word of God, and faith in God because of that word, there is the totality of Christianity.*

That, of course, is a paradoxical statement. But I have put it like that to highlight the fundamental and essential character of our faith. The Christian life of faith, in both Old and New Testaments, and in the experience of believers down the centuries and across the world, is brought into being and nourished, and brought to maturity, by God's *word*.

In chapter 2 we looked at the objection that this is too narrow a view of how God works—that it neglects the work of the Spirit. We saw that God's word comes to us by God's Spirit or breath, just as (forgive the foolish analogy) my words come to you by my breath. That makes them *my* words.

GOD OF WORD

In this final chapter we come to a question that, in a sense, should have been first on our agenda. What *is* this 'word of God'?

Does 'the Word of God' mean 'the Bible'?

Is it correct to assume—as I may seem to have done—that 'the word of God' simply means 'the Bible'?

We should not move too quickly to that identification. It is not as obvious as we might assume. Certainly in the Bible the phrase 'the word of God' does not always mean 'the Bible'. When Paul said, "Take the sword of the Spirit, which is the word of God", he did not mean "Pick up your Bibles"!

The issue here is not whether the Bible is the word of God. Upon that most of us agree. But at the present time there is an uneasiness with the proposition that the word of God is, for us, *no more* than the Bible. What if God *is* speaking other things, not, of course, at odds with the Bible, but nevertheless independent of the Bible? Are we guilty of quenching the Spirit and rejecting prophecy if the only word of God we hear is the Bible? Do we really have all of Christianity where there is only the *Bible* word of God, and the faith in God *it* brings about?

The question, in other words, has to do with

3. WORD AND BIBLE

the *sufficiency* of Scripture. This is the issue that gave rise to Martin Luther's slogan *sola scriptura*—Scripture alone: that not only is Scripture the word of God, but *only* Scripture is the word of God. This is a much-neglected issue, which has received very little recent attention from evangelicals. What is the basis and what are the implications of the Reformers' view that the word of God is the Bible and the Bible alone?

It depends what you mean by…

We need to begin by clarifying our terms. Before we ask, "Is God speaking new words today?", we need to work out what we mean by "God speaking". An illustration might help.

Suppose a Christian friend says to me, "I think your sermons are too long". Is God speaking to me? Since God is in control of all things, they are certainly the words he wants me to hear at that moment. Is it God's will that I take notice and shorten my sermons? Could well be! God is certainly accomplishing his purposes by controlling speaking events, because he is accomplishing his purposes by controlling all events. However, it *may* be more pleasing to God if I take up with my friend his slack attitude to the

GOD OF WORD

teaching of the Bible—and keep preaching just as long. That is at least a possibility!

Is God speaking new words today? It depends somewhat on what you mean by God speaking. What would not be right, however, is to describe my friend's wise and helpful comment as 'the word of God'.

There is an event in the New Testament that illustrates this point. In Acts 21:4 we find that some Christians in Tyre "through the Spirit... were telling Paul *not* to go on to Jerusalem". But Paul was not disobedient to God when he *did* go on to Jerusalem. These words, which in some sense were through the Spirit, were not what the New Testament calls 'the word of God'. The word of God is, as Peter put it, "the good news that was preached to you" (1 Pet 1:25). It is what is elsewhere called 'the gospel'.

So we must ask another question.

What does the Bible mean by 'the word of God'?

This is an important and not a self-evident question. What *did* Paul have in mind when he wrote "take the sword of the Spirit"? If he didn't mean "pick up your Bibles", neither did he have in mind something vague and indefinable. He (and his readers) knew what he meant. And it was clear and precise.

3. WORD AND BIBLE

1. 'The word about God' and 'the word from God'
Firstly, the phrase 'the Word of God' can have two senses. Both of these are to be found in the New Testament. It is the word *about* God, but it is also the word *from* God. In some contexts one of these senses will be more important than the other.

2. 'The word of God' is the apostolic gospel
In the New Testament 'the word of God' is that which *has been received from the apostles* (see such texts as Acts 6:2, 11:1, 18:11; Col 1:25). That is the word of God that is the sword of the Spirit. That is the word of God that Paul says *is* at work in the Thessalonian believers (1 Thess 2:13). The word of God is, as Peter put it, "the good news that was preached to you" (1 Pet 1:25).

3. 'The word of God' is a given, known message
There is, from the earliest New Testament writings, a sense of 'givenness' about the word of God. It is a message that the apostles realize they have received, and which they authoritatively pass on (1 Cor 15:3ff). This is what they call 'the word of God'.

It is the same throughout the Bible. There are moments of history when God makes known his purposes, when he reveals his grace—moments when he *speaks*. He spoke his promise to Abraham and restated and expanded it at Mount Sinai. He spoke his promise to David. He spoke through the prophets. Indeed:

> Long ago, at many times and in many ways, God spoke to our fathers by the prophets, but in these last days he has spoken to us by his Son… (Heb 1:1-2)

And God's word once spoken does not fade away, but remains and accomplishes his purposes (Isa 55:11). Once spoken, it is addressed not just to those who first heard it, but to succeeding generations—and just as immediately and directly to them as it was to the original hearers (we saw that especially in Deuteronomy 4 in chapter 1). Note how the author of Hebrews introduces Old Testament quotations with "The Holy Spirit *says*…"—present tense (Heb 3:7; cf. 9:8, 10:15-17).

The New Testament repeatedly speaks of the word of God in this sense—a word that is known, a word that has been received, yet by the work of God's Spirit a word that continues to be at work. This is the "sword of the Spirit", the word that brings about new birth, the word that calls forth faith in its hearers.

3. WORD AND BIBLE

4. 'The word of god' received from the apostles is complete

Now the question is: Is *this word of God that was received from the apostles complete*? The New Testament is very clear:

> But we ought always to give thanks to God for you, brothers beloved by the Lord, because God chose you as the firstfruits to be saved, through sanctification by the Spirit and belief in *the truth*. To this he called you through *our gospel*, so that you may obtain the glory of our Lord Jesus Christ. So then, brothers, stand firm and hold to *the traditions that you were taught by us, either by our spoken word or by our letter*. (2 Thess 2:13-15)

The words in italics refer to what Paul goes on, in 3:1, to call "the word of the Lord":

> Finally, brothers, pray for us, that *the word of the Lord* may speed ahead and be honoured, as happened among you...

This word has been given, indeed entrusted:

> O Timothy, guard *the deposit entrusted to you*... (1 Tim 6:20)

GOD OF WORD

> But I am not ashamed, for I know whom I have believed, and I am convinced that he is able to guard until that Day *what has been entrusted to me*. Follow the pattern of *the sound words that you have heard from me*, in the faith and love that are in Christ Jesus. By the Holy Spirit who dwells within us, guard *the good deposit* entrusted to you. (2 Tim 1:12b-14)

Of an overseer we read:

> He must hold firm to *the trustworthy word as taught*, so that he may be able to give instruction in sound doctrine and also to rebuke those who contradict. (Titus 1:9)

John wrote:

> Everyone who goes on ahead and does not abide in the teaching of Christ, does not have God. Whoever abides in the teaching has both the Father and the Son. (2 John 9)

And Jude:

> Beloved, although I was very eager to write to you about our common salvation, I found it necessary to write appealing to you to contend for the faith that *was once for all delivered to the saints*. (Jude 3)

3. WORD AND BIBLE

In other words, within the New Testament it is clear that this word of God is now complete, at least "until that Day". We cannot add to this word for the totality of Christianity, any more than we can add to Christ. *Where there is this word of God, and faith in God because of it, there is the totality of Christianity.*

5. God continues to speak *that* word

The New Testament is clear that in the Christian's experience God will continue to speak. But the word he speaks is not something new. We receive the word of the apostles "as what it really is, the word *of God*" (1 Thess 2:13). It is *that* word that is at work in you who believe. It is the gospel. It is the message of Christ crucified, risen, ascended.

What about the Bible?

The word of God once received, and written down, continues to be the living word of the living God—thanks to the work of the Holy Spirit. This is a thoroughly familiar idea in the Bible itself.

The Bible exists precisely because there were those who heeded the apostolic injunction to guard what had been entrusted to them by the Holy Spirit. As we have seen, in the Bible the phrase 'the word of

God' does not always mean 'the Bible'. But the Bible is the word of God. And it is complete.

To suggest that there is more to the word of God than the Bible is to suggest that there is more to the word of God than that which was entrusted to the apostles (an idea contrary to the New Testament) or that they failed to pass on adequately their trust (which is contrary to the evidence).

The question "Is there more to the word of God than the Bible?" can now be seen in a proper light: *Is there more to Christ than the apostolic gospel that has been delivered to us in the Bible?*

Do we really have all of Christianity where there is only the word of the Bible and the faith in God that it brings about? You might as well ask: Do we really have all of Christianity when we have all of Christ?

Conclusions

Let me finish with three concluding thoughts.

Firstly, Christian life and ministry will be marked by faith in God created by his word. It will only be possible to persist in such a ministry by that *faith*. The latest counselling technique or church growth formula will be a challenge to that faith. We are tempted to put our trust in all manner of alternatives

3. WORD AND BIBLE

to the word of God. That temptation has always been, and always will be, with us.

Secondly, the Christian life and ministry will be marked by *prayer*. It is the word *of God* that I have heard, and which is at work in me. If I believe that, I will pray.

Thirdly, it is the word *of God* that is the source of our faith and the content of our ministry. *All things* must be subordinated to the goal of seeing the word of God heard and understood and believed.

Feedback on this resource

We really appreciate getting feedback about our resources—not just suggestions for how to improve them, but also positive feedback and ways they can be used. We especially love to hear that the resources may have helped someone in their Christian growth.

You can send feedback to us via the 'Feedback' menu in our online store, or write to us at info@matthiasmedia.com.au.

Matthias Media is an evangelical publishing ministry that seeks to persuade all Christians of the truth of God's purposes in Jesus Christ as revealed in the Bible, and equip them with high-quality resources, so that by the work of the Holy Spirit they will:

- abandon their lives to the honour and service of Christ in daily holiness and decision-making
- pray constantly in Christ's name for the fruitfulness and growth of his gospel
- speak the Bible's life-changing word whenever and however they can—in the home, in the world and in the fellowship of his people.

Our resources range from Bible studies and books through to training courses, audio sermons and children's Sunday School material. To find out more, and to access samples and free downloads, visit our website:

www.matthiasmedia.com

How to buy our resources

1. Direct from us over the internet:
   – in the US: www.matthiasmedia.com
   – in Australia: www.matthiasmedia.com.au

2. Direct from us by phone: please visit our website for current phone contact information.

> Register at our website for our **free** regular email update to receive information about the latest new resources, **exclusive special offers**, and free articles to help you grow in your Christian life and ministry.

3. Through a range of outlets in various parts of the world. Visit **www.matthiasmedia.com/contact** for details about recommended retailers in your part of the world, including www.thegoodbook.co.uk in the United Kingdom.

4. Trade enquiries can be addressed to:
   – in the US and Canada: sales@matthiasmedia.com
   – in Australia and the rest of the world: sales@matthiasmedia.com.au

5. Visit **GoThereFor.com** for subscription-based access to a great-value range of digital resources.

More Brief Books from Matthias Media

The Everlasting Purpose

In just under 50 pages, Broughton Knox provides an extraordinarily clear and encouraging explanation of the Bible's teaching on predestination. He shows the comfort, assurance and blessing that flow from understanding the nature of God, the nature of man, and the means of our salvation in Christ.

Fearing God

Fear is taboo in Western society. Fear curtails freedom; it crushes dreams; it inhibits people. It should be avoided altogether. But some kinds of fear are healthy—just as some kinds of fearlessness are foolish. There is bad fear and good fear. In this short book, David Mears takes us back to the Bible to look again at the fear of God—and, more than that, to take delight in it and discover why it means we no longer have to be afraid.

How to Walk Into Church

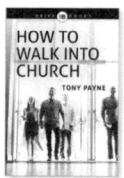

If you've been a churchgoer for more than just a few Sundays, walking into church probably doesn't seem like it deserves its own 'how to' manual. Right? It seems like a pretty straightforward and trivial weekly activity. But things are rarely as simple as they seem, and how you walk into church reveals a great deal about what you think church is, what it's for, and what you think you're doing there.

In *How to Walk into Church*, Tony Payne helps us think biblically about church. Along with giving plenty of other practical advice, he suggests a way to walk into church that beautifully expresses what church is and why you're there—a way that every Christian can master.

For more information or to order contact:

Matthias Media
Email: sales@matthiasmedia.com.au
www.matthiasmedia.com.au

Matthias Media (USA)
Email: sales@matthiasmedia.com
www.matthiasmedia.com